Clever Banners, PANELS & POSTCARDS

Mary

American Quilter's Society
P. O. Box 3290 • Paducah, KY 42002-3290
www.AmericanQuilter.com

D1416401

Located in Paducah, Kentucky, the American Quilter's Society (AQS) is dedicated to promoting the accomplishments of today's quilters. Through its publications and events, AQS strives to honor today's quilt-makers and their work and to inspire future creativity and innovation in quiltmaking.

EDITOR: TONI TOOMEY
TECHNICAL EDITOR: BARBARA SMITH
GRAPHIC DESIGN: ELAINE WILSON
COVER DESIGN: MICHAEL BUCKINGHAM
PHOTOGRAPHY: CHARLES R. LYNCH
HOW-TO-PHOTOGRAPHY: DAN MAYNE

LIBRARY OF CONGRESS CATALOGING-IN-PUBLICATION DATA

Mayne, Mary.

Clever banners, panels & postcards / by Mary Mayne.

p.cm.

Summary: "Postcards are taken to a new level with these mini-panels of various sizes complete with batting, backing, and binding. Make personalized gifts such as potholders, gift labels and birthday cards. Panels combine to make larger pieces. Embellishment notes and step-by-step guide for making a wallhanging provided" -- Provided by publisher.

ISBN 1-57432-911-1

1. Quilting--Patterns. 2. Patchwork--Patterns. 3. Miniature quilts. I. Title.
TT835.M3894 2006
746.46'041--dc22

2006025182

Additional copies of this book may be ordered from the American Quilter's Society, PO Box 3290, Paducah, KY 42002-3290; 800-626-5420 (orders only please); or online at www.AmericanQuilter.com. For all other inquiries, call 270-898-7903.

Proudly printed and bound in the United States of America

Dedication

To my husband, Peter, and my family, who supported me through the process of writing this book. Thank you for listening and encouraging me when I had my doubts. You will have my love forever.

Contents

Introduction

We all know as quilters that having the exact amount of fabric for a full-sized quilt never really happens. At the end of a project, scraps, or even large pieces, are always added to our stashes. I have always loved making things from these scraps, because I can honestly say that it doesn't cost me anything. The batting scraps cut from the edges of the larger quilts are also useful, especially for making small quilts. With this in mind, I began to think of wallhangings that might use up the small pieces, and postcard quilts and panels were born.

The first thing I did was draw a plan for a panel onto graph paper. Each square represented one inch. By doing this, I could easily work out the sizes for each postcard quilt. Drawing the designs for the postcards was easy because I could get inspiration from things I had around the house. We all have crackers, gifts, candles—the list is really endless!

Once the graph plan and the drawings were done, I began the exciting part — making the postcard quilts. I had great fun rummaging through my boxes of scraps to find the right fabrics. My first postcards had a Christmas theme. I didn't even need holiday fabrics. I realized, as long as I used seasonal shades and colors, I could still make a panel that had that Christmas glow. I then began to think of other themes for postcard panels. The next panel to be planned was for the most important room in the house. Yes, you've guessed. It's the sewing room. I ONLY WENT OUT FOR A FAT QUARTER was planned and made. CREAM TEAS was next.

With each project in this book, I will guide you through the stages of making postcard quilts and give you tips on embellishment. I am sure that you will feel the excitement just as I did in the beginning. I still have ideas waiting to be made, so my life is full, and I am ready for the next stage. I do hope you enjoy these projects as much as I have in designing and making them for my own home.

MAKING A POSTCARD QUILT

The following instructions take you through the steps for using fusible web and making the individual postcard quilts. With each pattern, I have given the requirements list, embellishment notes, and a step-by-step guide for sewing the postcard quilts into the full-sized panel.

Accuracy in your cutting and piecing is essential for your postcard quilts to fit together. I always use a ¼" seam allowance in my work. Some machines have a very accurate ¼" guide, and others have guides that are not as accurate. However, the quilts will go together just as well, so long as you always use the same seam allowance width throughout.

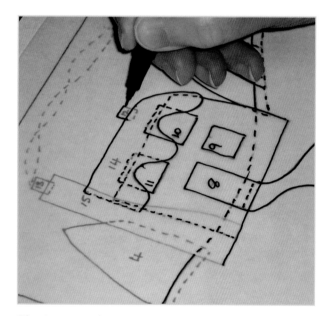

Fig. 1

PREPARING APPLIQUÉ PIECES

1. Use a black pen or fine-point permanent marker to trace the pattern from the book onto a sheet of tracing paper to make a master pattern. Be sure to trace the dotted lines that show where the pieces will overlap in the postcard (fig. 1).

> ### The Wrong Side Can Be the Right Side
> Don't be afraid to use the wrong side of a fabric if you think it works better than the right side. I do this often.

2. Now turn the master pattern over and work from the back. Trace each numbered piece in the master pattern onto the smooth paper backing of the fusible web, leaving a small gap between the shapes. Number each piece as shown on the master pattern (fig. 2).

3. Cut out each of these shapes, again leaving a small margin around the pencil line (fig. 3).

4. Place each shape, rough adhesive side down, onto the wrong side of your chosen fabrics. Press in place with a hot iron (fig. 4).

5. Cut out each shape on the drawn pencil line (fig. 5).

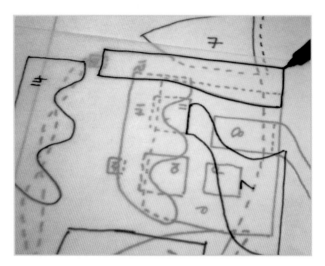
Fig. 2

Take It One Postcard at a Time
To avoid getting the pieces mixed up, make only one postcard at a time.

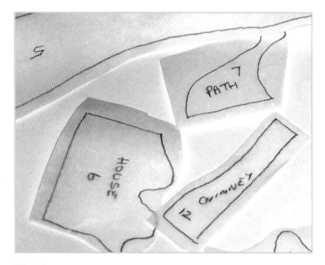
Fig. 3

Fig. 4

Fig. 5

Fig. 6

Fig. 7

Fig. 8

FUSING YOUR POSTCARD DESIGN

Next to my sewing machine, the Teflon® sheet is my best friend in my workroom. It's an invaluable piece of equipment when you are building up a design for fused appliqué. When you place this opaque-white, non-stick sheet over a master pattern, you can see the pattern through it. Teflon sheets can be purchased from most quilters' supply shops. I have had ladies in my workshops bring the Teflon sheets from the supermarket. Those are black or dark brown and not suitable for our purposes.

1. Turn your master pattern right side up and place the Teflon sheet over the pattern. Tape the sheet down if you like (fig. 6).

2. Take your first appliqué piece, peel off the paper backing, and place it on the Teflon sheet, adhesive side down, over the corresponding piece in the master pattern (fig. 7.). Peel the paper backing off the next shape and place it on the Teflon sheet. Lightly press the pieces to the Teflon sheet.

3. Continue in this way until all the pieces have been placed on the Teflon sheet (fig. 8).

4. Press the finished design with your iron and let it cool before peeling the whole design off the Teflon sheet (fig. 9). If the postcard has small pieces, such as holly berries, these can be

> ### *The Patterns Aren't Really Backward*
> You will be tracing the mirror images of what you will see on the finished quilt. Don't be worried about this. It will all work out, as you will see.

placed after the main pieces have been pressed on the background. Some of the postcards have only one shape. These can be placed directly on the background fabric without using the master pattern as a guide.

5. Position the design on your background fabric and iron it in place (fig. 10).

6. Sew the appliqué pieces in place with a straight stitch ⅛" from the edges (fig. 11).

Fig. 9

Choices for Stitching Your Design

You have a choice of methods for sewing the designs in place. I use the straight stitch on the sewing machine and a dark thread. If you use a black thread, it will make the design stand out and look as if you have drawn it and colored it in. You can hand sew the shapes using a small running stitch or a blanket stitch.

Another option is to use the blanket stitch on your machine. Remember that a lot of the pieces are so small that using this stitch would be quite difficult. Using the zigzag stitch would also be difficult. Whichever method you use, sew the pieces ⅛" from their raw edges.

I am often asked if it is possible to add the batting, backing, and borders to the postcard quilt before sewing around the shapes. I don't like this method, because it changes the appearance of the postcard. However, you can try layering then quilting one postcard quilt to see if you like it.

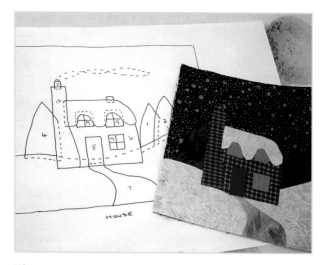
Fig. 10

Fig. 11

Fig. 12

Fig. 13

Fig. 14

FINISHING YOUR POSTCARD

As with most quilts, you add the borders before you add the batting and backing to the postcard. Make the borders from fabrics that are darker than your background fabric. The border fabrics can be any color: print, check, striped, or solid. Scraps are ideal for borders. Use a different fabric for each side of a postcard. Try to plan your panel or banner so you won't be placing two borders with the same fabric side by side when you piece the whole panel together.

Most of the borders are cut from 1" strips. Some of the projects, however, have borders cut from 1½" strips. Be sure to check the project instructions before cutting the border strips.

Important: It is important to cut all four border strips to the exact length before sewing them to the postcard. This will help your postcards stay square at the corners. If you sew long strips and then trim off the excess, there is a tendency for the corners to curve over slightly. The strip lengths for each postcard are based on the width and height of the postcard's background and the width of the strip.

1. Cut all four strips to the lengths given in the project instructions (fig. 12).

2. Sew the border strips on one at a time, beginning with the top strip and working clockwise around the postcard. Press each strip to the right side before sewing the next strip (fig. 13).

3. To layer your postcard quilt, place the batting on the bottom, then put the backing right-side up on top of the batting. Position the postcard face down on the backing (fig. 14).

Note: Layering and finishing your postcard quilt is unlike the method you would normally use to finish a traditional quilt.

4. Pin and baste the three layers together. Because these quilts are so small, I put pins in the corners and around the sides (fig. 15).

5. With a walking foot on your machine, sew around the border ¼" from the edge. Leave a small opening along one side for turning the quilt right side out. Trim off the excess batting and backing, and trim the corners (fig. 16).

6. Turn the postcard quilt through the opening to the right side. Ease the corners out, and slip stitch the opening closed (fig. 17).

7. Machine or hand quilt around the inside edge of the borders and around the appliquéd shape if you like. You can add embellishments at this stage.

Your postcard quilt is now finished as a complete work of art. Make as many as you like and build up the complete collection for whichever mini panel you are making.

ASSEMBLING A BANNER

Each project has a panel assembly diagram that shows you the order for sewing the postcard quilts together. Follow these diagrams and you can't go wrong.

1. Place your first two postcard quilts together back to back. Use pearl cotton or embroidery thread to sew the edges with a large overcast stitch (fig. 18, page 12). Finish off with two or three overcast stitches on the back of the joined quilts.

Fig. 15

Fig. 16

Fig. 17

Fig. 18

Fig. 19

Note: Try not to sew the stitches too tightly or too loosely.

2. Continue sewing the postcard quilts together according to the panel assembly diagram. When two postcards are sewn together, gently pull the postcards to make them lie flat before adding the next one (fig. 19).

Another Way to Assemble a Panel

In each of the projects for this book, I made individual postcard quilts and then sewed them together. If you like, you can sew all the postcards together as you would the blocks in a traditional quilt and then add the batting and backing and quilt in the traditional way.

Patterns

Mailing Your Postcard Quilt

A postcard quilt made with regular batting will require First Class letter rates. To qualify for letter rates, your quilt can be no smaller than 3½" x 5", no larger than 6⅛" x 11½", and no thicker than ¼".

To mail your quilt as a postcard, in place of batting, use a firm interfacing, such as Pelex®. To qualify for postcard rates, your quilt must be no smaller than 3½" x 5" and no larger than 4¼" x 6". Draw a line down the middle of the back of the quilt, and write Postcard on the top, then use one side for the address and one side for your message.

The stamps on a quilt must be glued on and hand cancelled. Take your quilt to the Post Office, where they can weigh it, sell you the stamps you need for it, and hand cancel them. Be sure to take some glue to hold the stamps on the quilt.

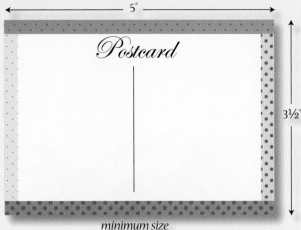

minimum size

THREE HENS A-LAYING, 23½" x 19". Made by the author.

THREE HENS A-LAYING

panel size: 23½" x 19"

REQUIREMENTS

Postcard	Background
Chickens	5½" x 6½" Cut 3.
Roof	5" x 22" Then cut from template on page 19
Nests	3½" x 19½"

Additional Requirements

Appliqué fabrics. A lot of scraps are all you need. Include reds for chickens' wattles and combs, and yellow-orange for their beaks. Choose a check or woodgrain print for the roof background. Make your chickens as colorful as you like.

Embellishments: Use beads for the hens' eyes. Look for chicken pins, buttons, and beads for these postcards.

Border strips. Cut borders from 1½" strips.

Top border: Cut background width.

Right-side border: Add 1¼" to background height.

Bottom border: Add 1¼" to background width.

Left-side border: Add 2½" to background height.

Roof borders: Cut one strip 1½" x 18", two strips 1½" x 12", and one strip 1½" x 27".

Fusible web. Have ¾ yd. on hand.

Batting and Backing. Add 3" to background measurements.

SCRAP BAG OF IDEAS

Here are some other ways to use the THREE HENS A-LAYING postcards as embellishments and banners.

- This little panel is ideal for the kitchen.
- Appliqué chickens to tea towels or curtains.
- Add a few chickens to cushions for kitchen chairs.
- Use the hens to embellish covers for your kitchen appliances.

CONSTRUCTION TIPS

1. For general instructions, see Making a Postcard Quilt on pages 6–12.

2. Sew the borders to the postcard backgrounds before fusing the appliqué pieces. This will allow the nests to overlap the borders, as shown in the THREE HENS A-LAYING panel pictured on page 14.

3. After the Hen postcards are sewn together, you may need to trim the width of the nest background.

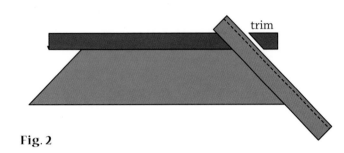

Fig. 1

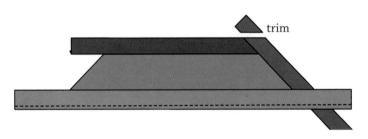

Fig. 2

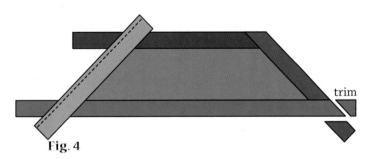

Fig. 3

Fig. 4

Adding the Hen House Roof Borders

The border strips are longer than needed. You can trim them after sewing them to the roof background.

1. Pin and sew the 1½" x 18" strip to the top edge of the roof background, then press the strip to the right side (fig. 1).

2. Sew a 12" strip to the right side of the roof background. Press the strip to the right side, and trim (fig. 2).

3. Sew the 27" strip to the bottom of the roof background. Press the strip to the right side and trim (fig. 3).

4. Sew a 12" strip to the left side of the roof background. Press the strip to the right side and trim (fig. 4).

FINISHING TIPS

1. Join the completed postcards according to the THREE HENS A-LAYING panel assembly diagram on page 17.

2. Sew a hanging sleeve to the back of your panel, then date and sign it.

HENHOUSE

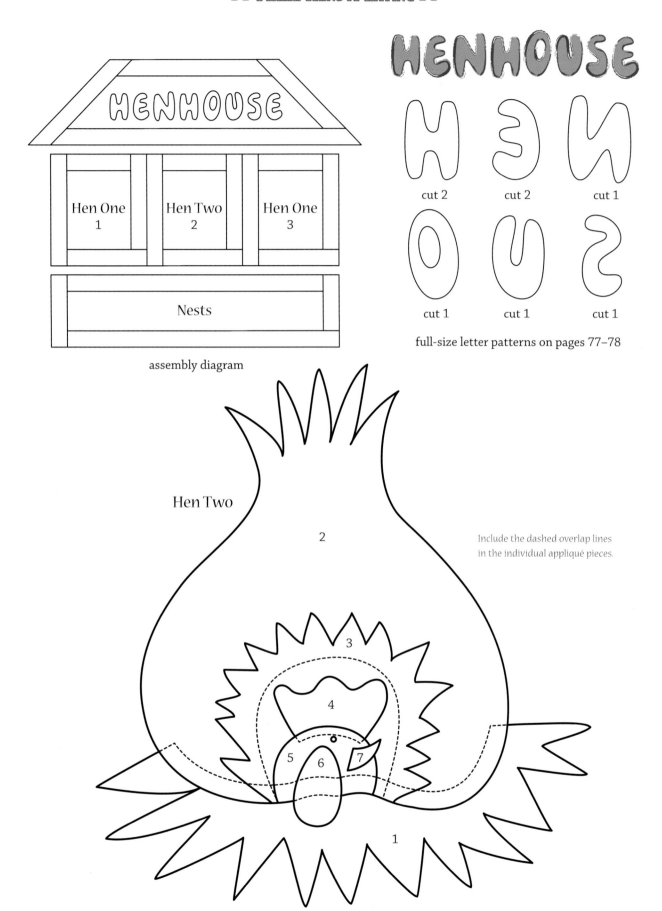

HENHOUSE

Hen One
1

Hen Two
2

Hen One
3

Nests

assembly diagram

cut 2   cut 2   cut 1

cut 1   cut 1   cut 1

full-size letter patterns on pages 77–78

Hen Two

2

Include the dashed overlap lines
in the individual appliqué pieces.

3

4

5   6   7

1

Include the dashed overlap lines in the individual appliqué pieces.

Hen One

Chick

Nest
cut 3

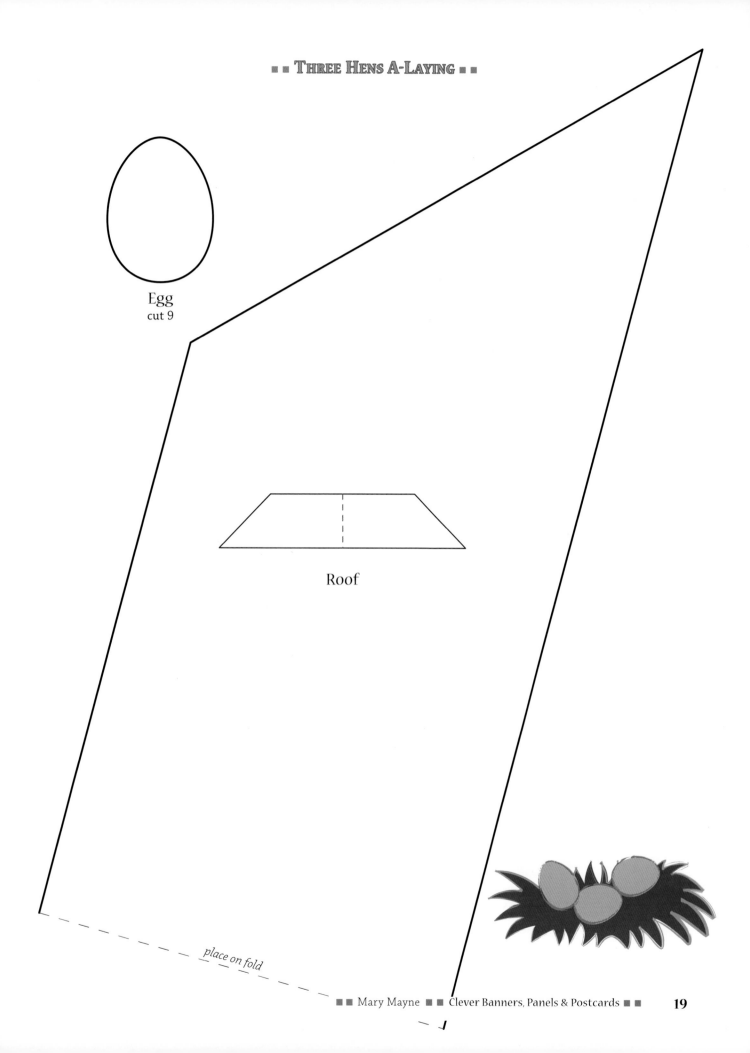

Egg
cut 9

Roof

place on fold

Fantasy Flowers, 16½" x 25". Made by the author.

FANTASY FLOWERS

panel size: 16½" x 25"

REQUIREMENTS

Postcard	Background
Flowers 1–6	4¼" x 11" Cut 6.

Additional Requirements

Appliqué fabrics. Scraps of spring pastels and vibrant, summery colors for the flowers. All kinds of greens for the leaves.

Embellishments. Hand embroider a blanket stitch around the petals in Flowers 1–5. Sew a machine straight stitch with *cordonnet* topstitching thread around the leaves. Use buttons for the centers of flowers 4 and 5.

Border strips. Cut borders from 1½" strips.

Top border: Cut background width.

Right-side border: Add 1¼" to background height.

Bottom border: Add 1¼" to background width.

Left-side border: Add 2½" to background height.

Fusible web. Have 1 yd. on hand.

Batting and Backing. Add 3" to background measurements.

SCRAP BAG OF IDEAS

Here are some other ways to use the FANTASY FLOWERS postcards as embellishments and banners.

- Fuse a flower on the front of a plain shirt. Put one on the back, too.
- Make small wallhangings with individual Flower postcards. Make banners of Flower postcards joined end-to-end or side-by-side.

CONSTRUCTION TIPS

1. For general instructions, see Making a Postcard Quilt on pages 6–12.

2. Hand embroider the stems on the backgrounds before fusing the flowers.

3. Hand embroider the petals in Flowers 1–5 with a blanket stitch after fusing them to the backgrounds.

4. After fusing, hand embroider with a blanket stitch around Flowers 1–3 and 6, and a running stitch around Flowers 4 and 5.

FINISHING TIPS

1. Join the completed postcards according to the FANTASY FLOWERS panel assembly diagram on page 22.

2. Sew a hanging sleeve to the back of your panel, then date and sign it.

assembly diagram

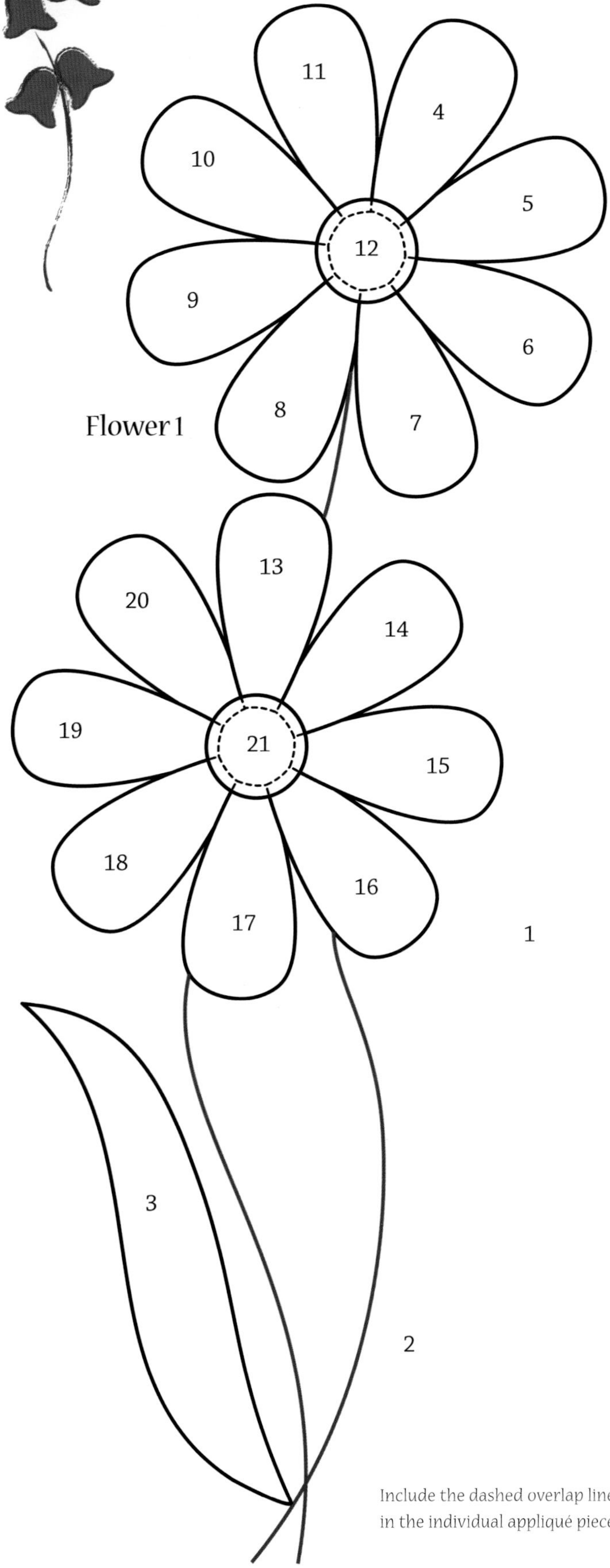

11

4

10

5

12

9

6

8

7

Flower 1

Flower 2

13

20

14

19

21

15

18

16

17

1

1

3

3

4

2

2

Include the dashed overlap lines
in the individual appliqué pieces.

Flower 3

1

1

2

2

1

2

1

2

Flower 4

Include the dashed overlap lines in the individual appliqué pieces.

3

4

5

6

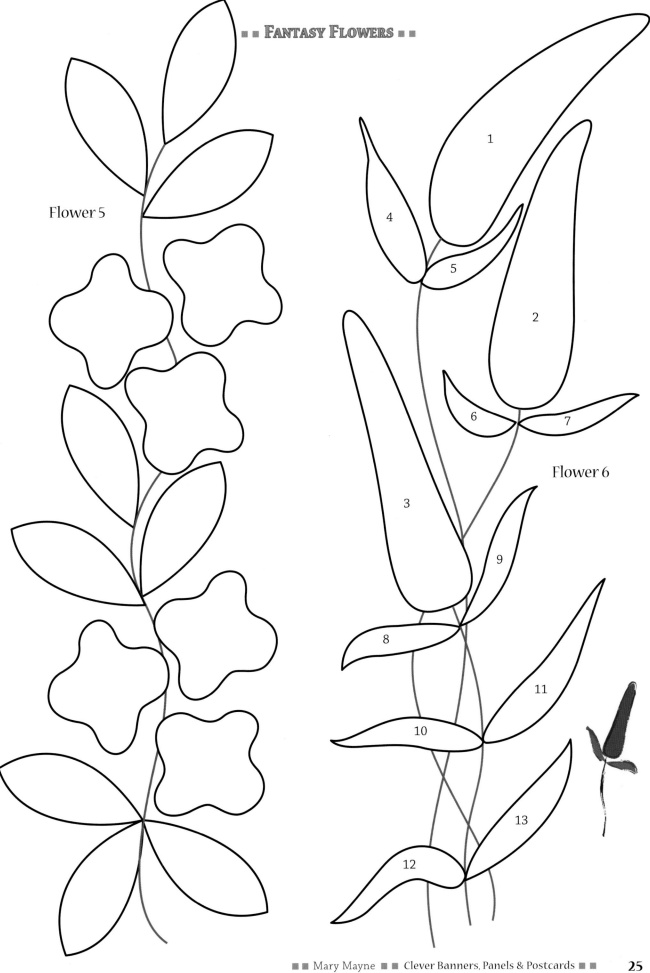

Flower 5

Flower 6

1

4

5

2

6

7

3

9

8

11

10

13

12

SUGAR AND SPICE, 17" x 23". Made by the author.

Sugar and Spice

panel size: 17" x 23"

REQUIREMENTS

Postcard	Background
Sugar and Spice	3½" x 16½"
All Things Nice	3½" x 16½"
Teddy	4½" x 6½"
1, 2, 3	2½" x 4½"
Flowers	3½" x 6½"
Balloons	4½" x 4½"
Alphabet Blocks	5½" x 6½"
Rag Doll	4½" x 6½"
Hearts	2½" x 4½"
Doll's Pram	4½" x 4½"
House	4½" x 6½"

Additional Requirements

Appliqué fabrics. This panel is for a little girl, so I used all pinks and creams, but any variety of soft colors will do.

Embellishments. I went through my buttons and beads and found lots of little things to add to this quilt: pink stars, a clock, a pink pencil button, and a clown face. I added tiny pink beads on the Rag Doll dress, and used white pearl buttons to make the centers of the Flowers. A white pearl heart is stitched to the Hearts postcard, and tiny pink buttons make the wheel hubs on the Doll's Pram. Hand embroider labels to any of the postcards you'd like, the way I did on the House and Doll's Pram postcards.

Border strips. Cut borders from 1" strips.

Top border: Cut background width.

Right-side border: Add ¾" to background height.

Bottom border: Add ¾" to background width.

Left-side border: Add 1½" to background height.

Fusible web. Have ¾ yd. on hand.

Batting and Backing. Add 2" to background measurements.

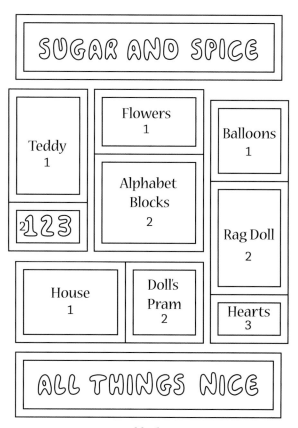

assembly diagram

SCRAP BAG OF IDEAS

Here are some other ways to use the SUGAR AND SPICE postcards as embellishments and banners.

■ You can do so much for a little girl's room with these designs: borders for curtains, appliqué on bed linens, a doll's quilt, cushions with rag doll and teddy. Let your imagination go.

CONSTRUCTION TIPS

1. For general instructions, see Making a Postcard Quilt on pages 6–12.

2. To embellish the rag doll's dress, machine sew a double line down the center of her dress, and sew three tiny pink beads at the top for her buttons. Draw her face with a marking pen or fabric marker. Use tiny beads for her eyes.

3. Appliqué the balloons and highlights in the Balloons postcard, then hand embroider the strings.

FINISHING TIPS

1. Join the completed postcards according to the SUGAR AND SPICE panel assembly diagram.

2. Sew a hanging sleeve to the back of your panel, then date and sign it.

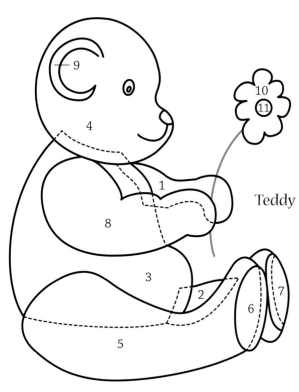

Teddy

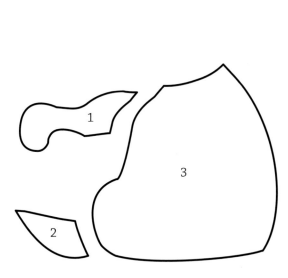

Trace directly on fusible-web backing.

Include the dashed overlap lines
in the individual appliqué pieces.

For you

Flowers

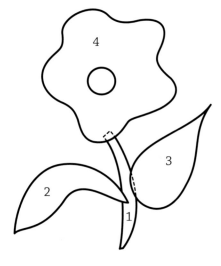

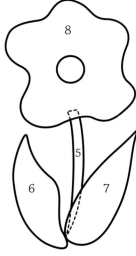

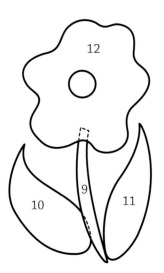

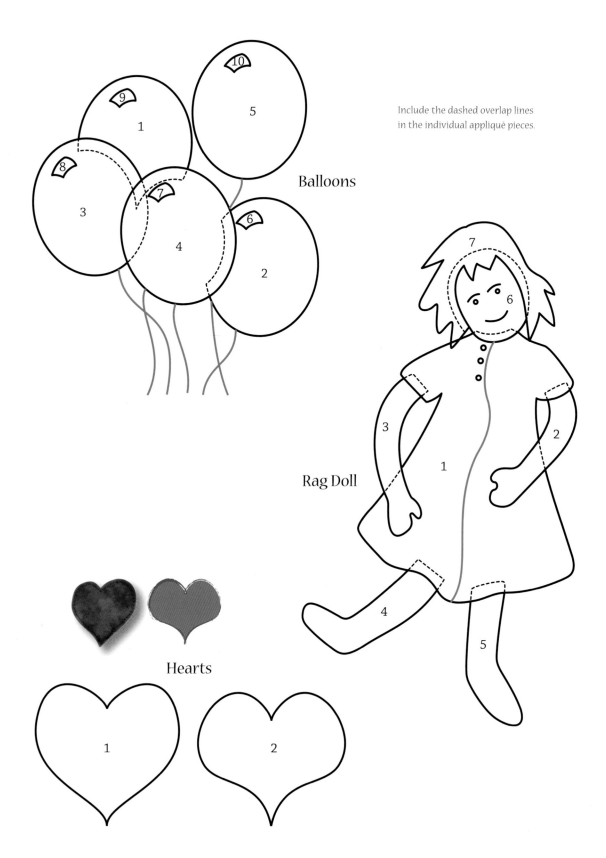

Include the dashed overlap lines
in the individual appliqué pieces.

Balloons

Rag Doll

Hearts

Trace directly on fusible-web backing.

HOUSE

House

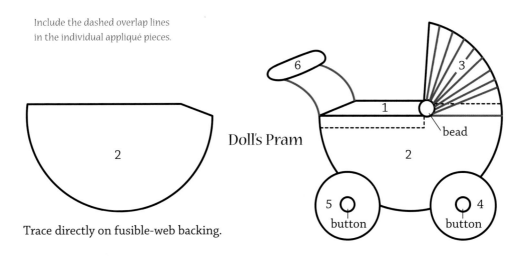

Numbers

Trace directly on fusible-web backing.

Include the dashed overlap lines in the individual appliqué pieces.

Doll's Pram

Trace directly on fusible-web backing.

full-size letter patterns on pages 77–78

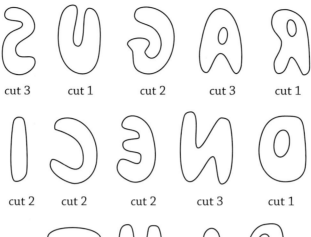

cut 3   cut 1   cut 2   cut 3   cut 1

cut 2   cut 2   cut 2   cut 3   cut 1

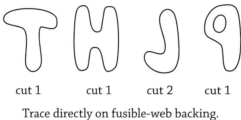

cut 1   cut 1   cut 2   cut 1

Trace directly on fusible-web backing.

Alphabet Blocks

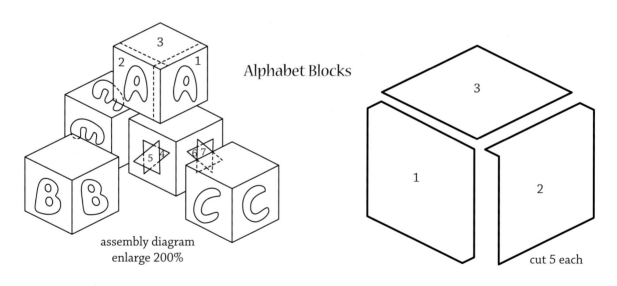

assembly diagram
enlarge 200%

cut 5 each

Trace directly on fusible-web backing.

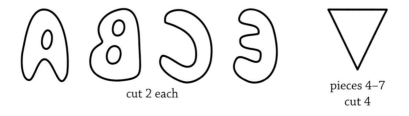

cut 2 each

pieces 4–7
cut 4

NOEL, 18" x 20½". Made by the author.

NOEL

panel size: 18"x 20½"

REQUIREMENTS

Postcard	Background
Tree	4½" x 9"
Pudding	5½" x 5½"
Gift	4" x 4"
Robin	4" x 4"
Rudolph	4½" x 6½"
Santa	4" x 5½"
Holly	4" x 2½"
Noel	8" x 2½"
Snowman	3½" x 7"
House	6½" x 5½"
Garland	17½" x 3½"

Additional Requirements

Appliqué pieces. A lot of scraps. Include reds, greens, golds, browns, black, and small prints in all colors.

Embellishments. Use tiny red beads for the flower centers in the garlands. Add a star sequin and a tiny bead in the sky in the House postcard, and machine stitch or hand embroider the smoke and window panes. Use tiny beads and buttons for the eyes and mouths in the postcards. In the Holly postcard, sew a red bead to hold each berry in place instead of machine stitching around them. Hang a little star from Rudolph's antler.

Border strips. Cut borders from 1" strips.

Top border: Cut background width.

Right-side border: Add ¾" to background height.

Bottom border: Add ¾" to background width.

Left-side border: Add 1½" to background height.

Fusible web. Have ¾ yd. on hand.

Batting and Backing. Add 2" to background measurements.

SCRAP BAG OF IDEAS

Here are some other ways to use the NOEL postcards as embellishments and banners.

■ Apply a row of Rudolphs around the hem of a holiday tablecloth.

■ Use Holly postcards as gift tags. Make the backing out of cream calico to write your greeting, and sew a ribbon on for the tie.

■ Make a holiday hanging for the kitchen out of six Pudding postcards.

■ Make a panel from a long row of Trees and a row of Snowman postcards.

■ Enlarge designs to make place mats for the table.

CONSTRUCTION TIPS

1. For general instructions, see Making a Postcard Quilt on pages 6–12.

2. Instead of trying to sew around the berries and other tiny pieces, fuse the pieces to the postcard, then anchor them in place with small beads.

3. Hand embroider the robin's beak and legs and use beads for the eyes.

FINISHING TIPS

1. Join the completed postcards according to the NOEL panel assembly diagram.

2. Sew a hanging sleeve to the back of your panel, then date and sign it.

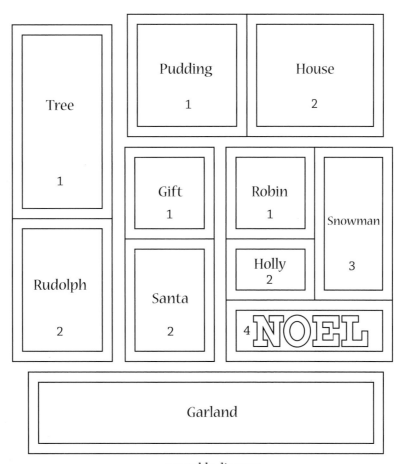

assembly diagram

Robin

bead

Tree

5

4

3

2

1

Trace directly on fusible-web backing.

Include the dashed overlap lines
in the individual appliqué pieces.

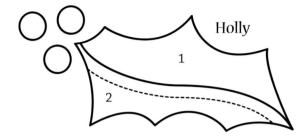

Holly

1

2

Include the dashed overlap lines
in the individual appliqué pieces.

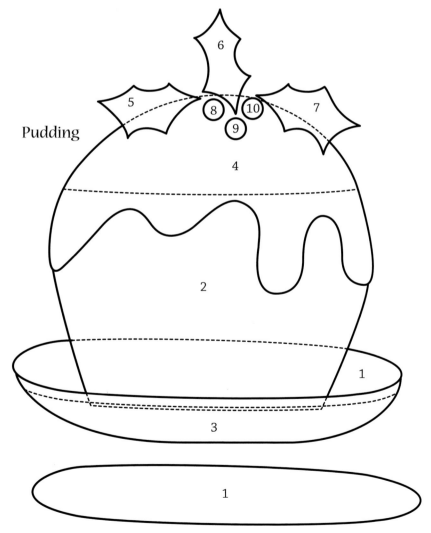

Pudding

6

5   8 10   7

9

4

2

1

3

1

Trace directly on fusible-web backing. Fuse to the right side of the fabric.

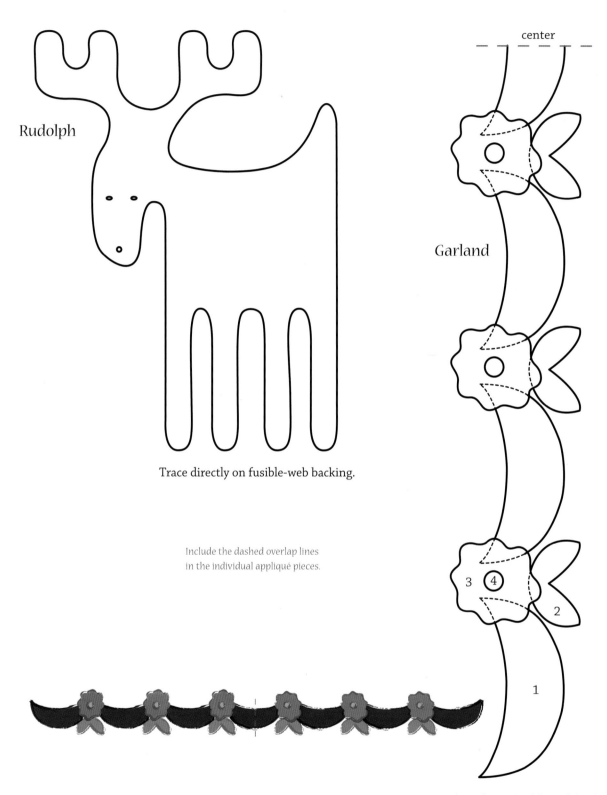

Rudolph

Trace directly on fusible-web backing.

Include the dashed overlap lines
in the individual appliqué pieces.

center

Garland

3 4

2

1

Trace directly on fusible-web backing.

Santa

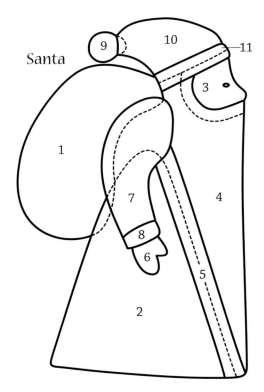

Include the dashed overlap lines
in the individual appliqué pieces.

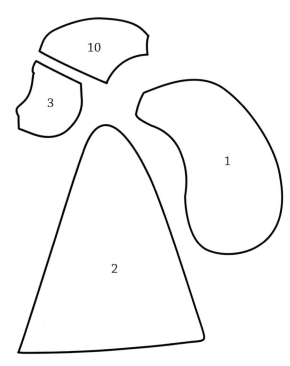

Trace directly on fusible-web backing.

Gift

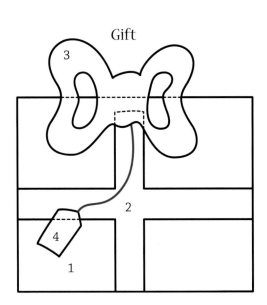

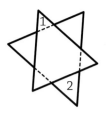

Snowman

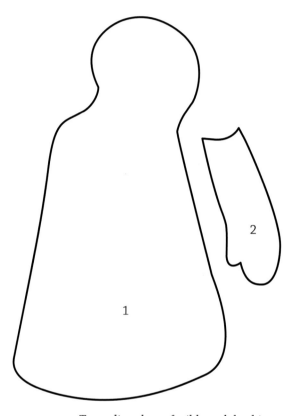

Include the dashed overlap lines
in the individual appliqué pieces.

Trace directly on fusible-web backing.

Noel

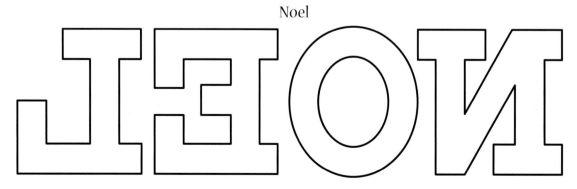

Trace directly on fusible-web backing.

Include the dashed overlap lines
in the individual appliqué pieces.

House

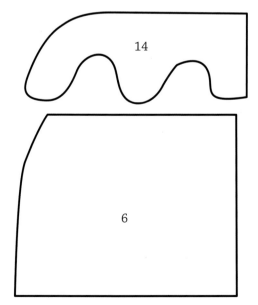

Trace directly on fusible-web backing.

Cream Teas, 14" x 26". Made by the author.

CREAM TEAS

panel size: 14"x 26"

REQUIREMENTS

Postcard	Background
Swiss Roll, Cream	6½" x 3½" Cut 2.
Sandwiches, Strawberries and Cream	9½" x 3½" Cut 2.
Ice Cream Sundae	9½" x 4½"
Fairy Cakes and Butterfly Cake	3½" x 3½" Cut 3.
Cup and Saucer	4½" x 3½"
Tea Pot	5½" x 5½"
Meringues	3½" x 7½"
Flower, Cherries	2½" x 2½" Cut 2.

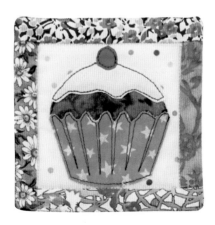

Additional Requirements

Appliqué pieces. A lot of scraps. Include pastels and a few reds for the cherries and strawberries, greens, and small prints in all colors.

Border strip. Cut borders from 1" strips.

Top border: Cut background width.

Right-side border: Add ¾" to background height.

Bottom border: Add ¾" to background width.

Left-side border: Add 1½" to background height.

Fusible web. Have ¾ yd. on hand.

Batting and Backing. Add 2" to background measurements.

SCRAP BAG OF IDEAS

Here are some other ways to use the CREAM TEAS postcards as embellishments and banners.

■ I have had great fun making Fairy Cake postcards, putting them in with birthday cards for friends.

■ The Cups and Saucers postcard design would look great on a tablecloth and napkins. A table cloth for tea in the garden would look fine with a mixture of Sandwiches and Strawberries and Cream appliquéd all over.

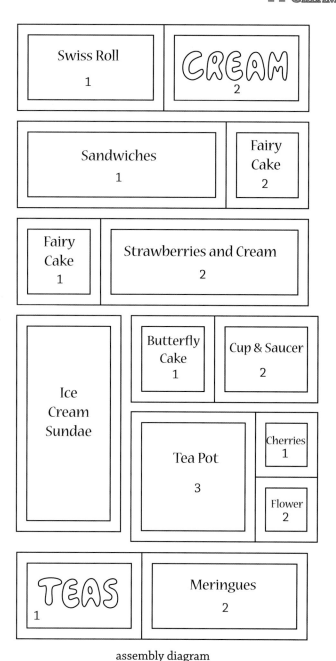

Swiss Roll	CREAM
1	2

Sandwiches	Fairy Cake
1	2

Fairy Cake	Strawberries and Cream
1	2

Ice Cream Sundae	Butterfly Cake	Cup & Saucer
	1	2
	Tea Pot	Cherries / 1
	3	Flower / 2

TEAS	Meringues
1	2

assembly diagram

CONSTRUCTION TIPS

1. For general instructions, see Making a Postcard Quilt on pages 6–12.

2. For each strawberry stem, hand sew one stitch through the top of the strawberry with green embroidery thread then tie a small knot

3. Draw the spiral on the Swiss Roll with a pencil, as shown in the pattern on page 45. Use a machine zigzag stitch to sew the spiral on the roll.

4. Use a machine straight stitch to draw ridges on the cupcake papers. Start at the upper left and sew as shown in the Fairy Cake and Butterfly Cake patterns on page 47.

FINISHING TIPS

5. Join the completed postcards according to the CREAM TEAS panel assembly diagram.

6. Sew a hanging sleeve to the back of your panel, then date and sign it.

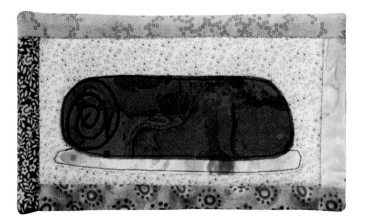

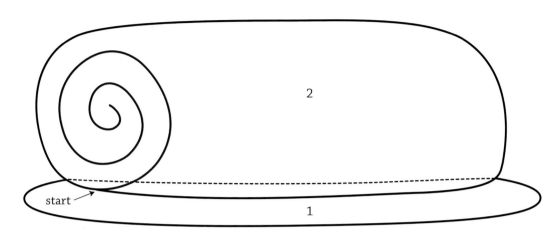

Swiss Roll

Include the dashed overlap lines
in the individual appliqué pieces.

Trace directly on fusible-web backing.

Strawberries and Cream

strawberry cut 9

Trace directly on fusible-web backing.

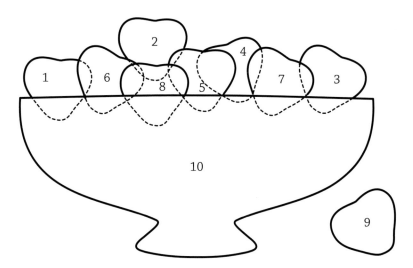

Include the dashed overlap lines
in the individual appliqué pieces.

Meringues

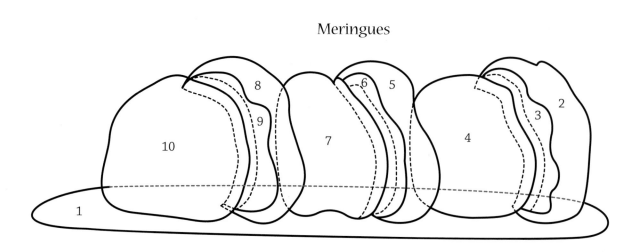

Sandwiches

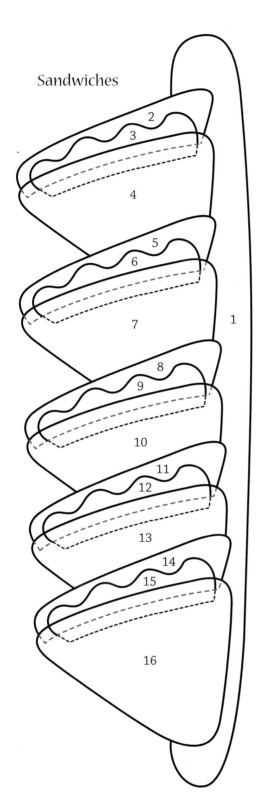

Fairy Cake

Butterfly Cake

Include the dashed overlap lines
in the individual appliqué pieces.

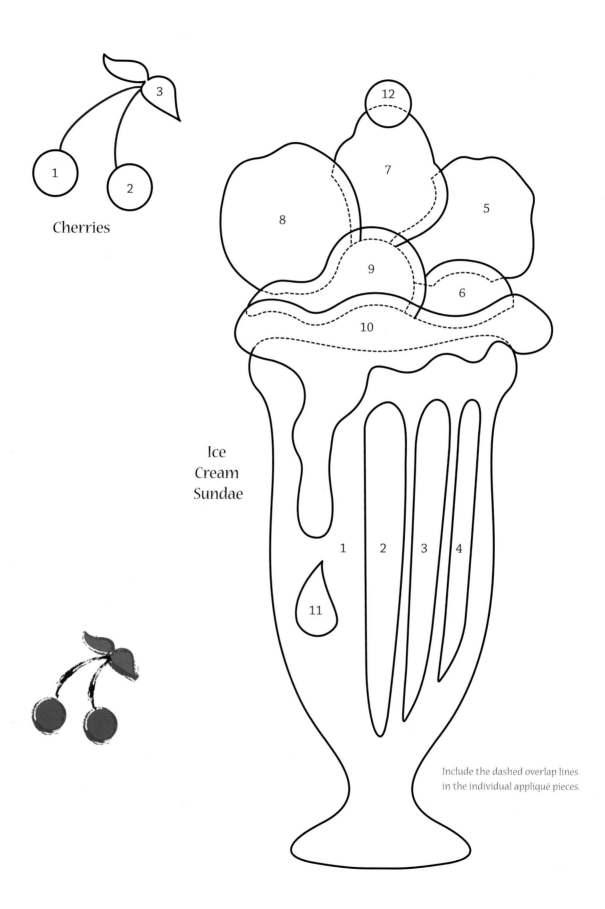

Cherries

Ice
Cream
Sundae

Include the dashed overlap lines
in the individual appliqué pieces.

Cup and
Saucer

Flower

Include the dashed overlap lines
in the individual appliqué pieces.

Trace pieces 1–8 directly on fusible-web backing.

Tea Pot

I ONLY WENT OUT FOR A FAT QUARTER, 30" x 14". Made by the author.

I Only Went Out for a Fat Quarter

panel size: 30" x 14"

REQUIREMENTS

Postcard	Background
Spools	4½" x 6½"
Cutter and Ruler	6½" x 6½"
Quilter	6½" x 11½"
Pin Cushion	4½" x 4½"
Scissors	4½" x 6½"
Sewing Machine	6½" x 6½"
Iron	4½" x 6½"

Additional Requirements

Appliqué fabrics. A lot of scraps. I used striped fabrics for the colors on the spools of thread in Spools

Embellishments. I used ceramic sewing-related buttons to add interest. I also used buttons for the controls on the Sewing Machine. Sew a tiny button at the hinge of the scissors blades. Use colored beads for the pinheads. In the Sewing Machine postcard, machine stitch the threads from the cotton spools and machine needle.

Border strips. Cut borders from 1½" strips.

Top border: Cut background width.

Right-side border: Add 1¼" to background height.

Bottom border: Add 1¼" to background width.

Left-side border: Add 2½" to background height.

Fusible web. Have 1 yd. on hand.

Batting and Backing. Add 2" to background measurements.

SCRAP BAG OF IDEAS

Here are some other ways to use the I Only Went Out for a Fat Quarter postcards as embellishments and banners.

■ These designs are ideal for cushion fronts. I have made two. One has the Sewing Machine design in the center, and the other has a group with the Pin Cushion, Scissors, and Spools designs.

■ Appliqué a row of sewing machines and spools to the hemline of sewing-room curtains.

CONSTRUCTION TIPS

1. For general instructions, see Making a Postcard Quilt on pages 6–12.

2. I have hand written the titles on some of the postcards with a Pigma® pen, but you can embroider the writing if you prefer.

FINISHING TIPS

1. Join the completed postcards according to the I ONLY WENT OUT FOR A FAT QUARTER panel assembly diagram.

2. Sew 6" squares of fabric to the bottom edge of the panel. I used different colored buttons to hold the squares on.

3. Sew a sleeve to the hanging and date and sign your panel.

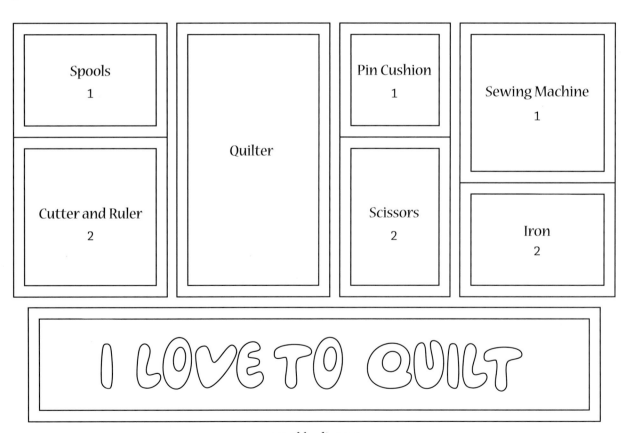

assembly diagram

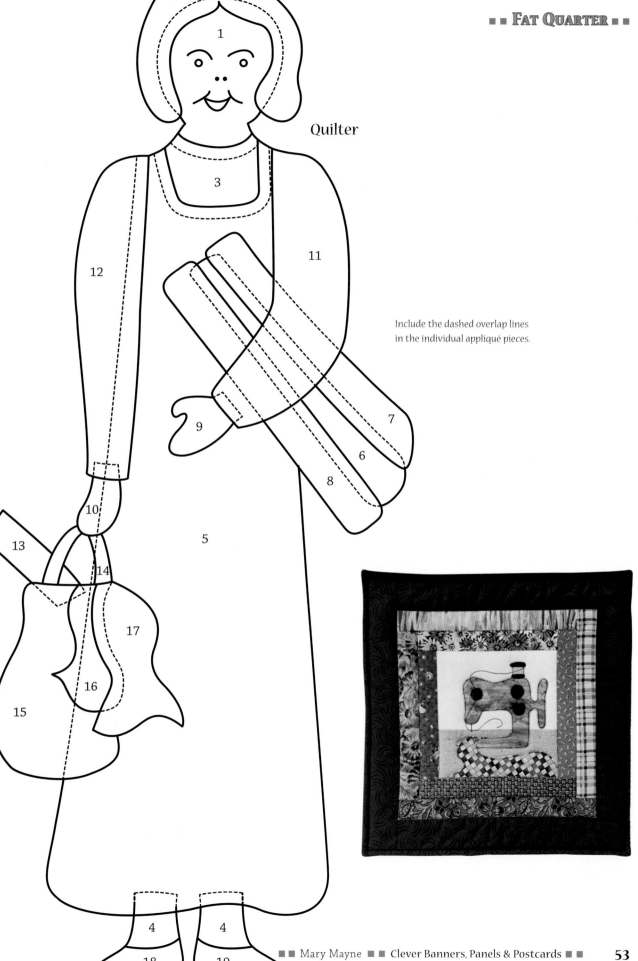

Quilter

Include the dashed overlap lines in the individual appliqué pieces.

Cutter and Ruler

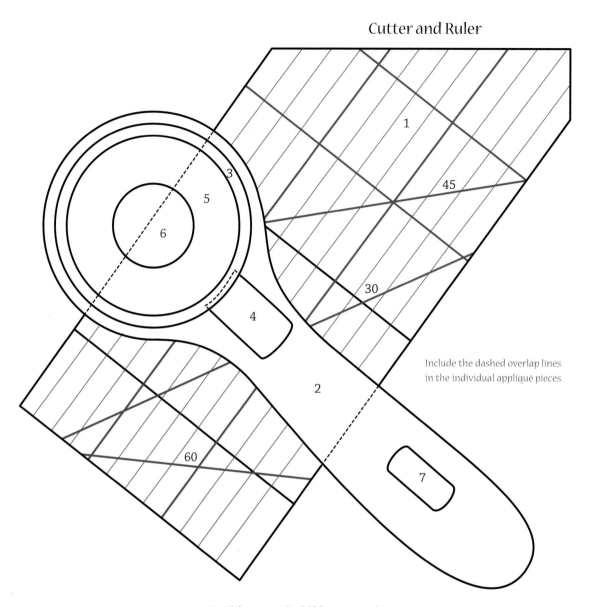

1

45

3

5

6

30

4

2

Include the dashed overlap lines in the individual appliqué pieces.

60

7

Use fabric pen for ¼" lines on ruler.

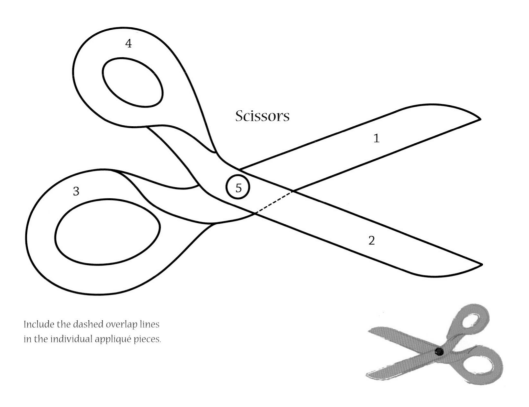

Scissors

Include the dashed overlap lines
in the individual appliqué pieces.

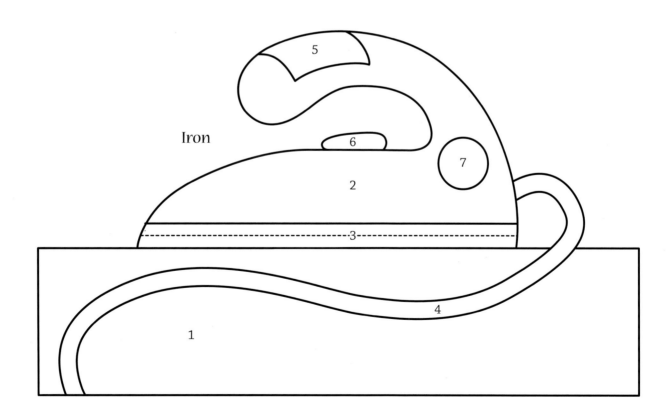

Iron

Pin Cushion

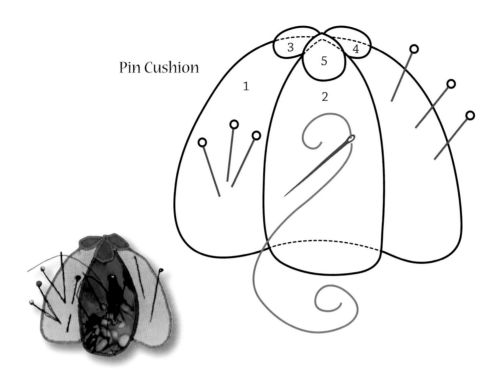

Spools

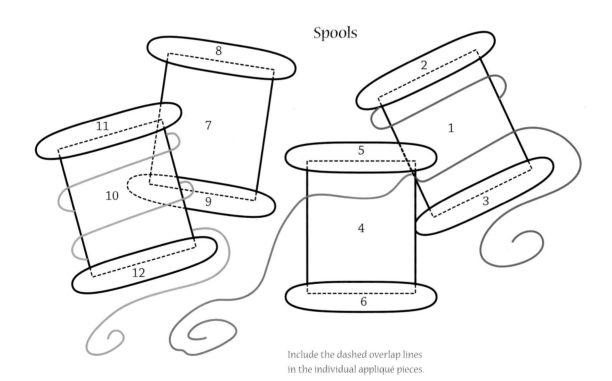

Include the dashed overlap lines
in the individual appliqué pieces.

enlarge letters 300%

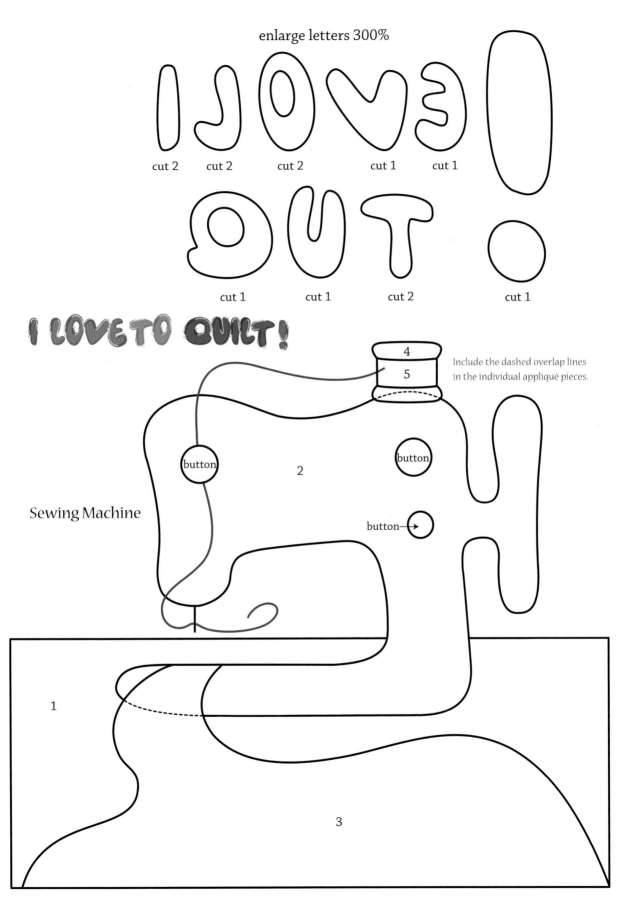

cut 2   cut 2   cut 2   cut 1   cut 1

cut 1   cut 1   cut 2   cut 1

I LOVE TO QUILT!

4

5

Include the dashed overlap lines
in the individual appliqué pieces.

button   2   button

Sewing Machine   button→

1

3

SPOOKY NIGHTS! 22" x 22". Made by the author.

SPOOKY NIGHTS!

panel size: 22" x 22"

REQUIREMENTS

Postcard	Background
Ghost	10½" x 10½"
Leaves	3½" x 10½"
Pumpkins	3½" x 15½"
Halloween	3½" x 15½"
Trick or Treat	3½" x 20½"

Additional Requirements

Appliqué fabrics. Use any scraps your stash has to offer. Use dark, spooky fabrics for the backgrounds.

Embellishments. Use beads and plastic spiders. (The real thing won't work!) My spiders are made of small black buttons. You can really have fun with this hanging. Use silver thread or gray thread for the spider web in the Ghost postcard.

Border strips. Cut borders from 1½" strips.

Top border: Cut background width.

Right-side border: Add 1¼" to background height.

Bottom border: Add 1¼" to background width.

Left-side border: Add 2½" to background height.

Fusible web. Have 1 yd. on hand.

Batting and Backing. Add 3" to background measurements.

SCRAP BAG OF IDEAS

Here are some other ways to use the SPOOKY NIGHTS! postcards as embellishments and banners.

■ Use the Pumpkins on Halloween table napkins and leaves around the tablecloth.

■ Appliqué the ghost and witch to a child's costume for trick-or-treating.

CONSTRUCTION TIPS

For general instructions, see the Making a Postcard Quilt on pages 6–12.

GHOST POSTCARD

1. Use the Ghost postcard assembly diagram on page 61 to construct the ghost block.

2. Cut away the mouth and eyes on piece 2.

3. Fuse pieces 1–4 to the Ghost background fabric.

4. Add the borders (labeled as pieces 5–8) so the remaining appliqué pieces can overlap them, as shown in the postcard pattern.

5. Finish fusing the pieces for the witch, then add the pumpkins. Machine stitch to embellish the pumpkins, as shown in the postcard pattern on page 61

6. Cut as many leaves as you like, and assemble as many ears of corn as you like. Then add the leaves and corn to the postcard.

7. Mark the spider web with white pencil, and machine stitch along the lines with silver or grey thread. My spider is a small black button with four holes. The legs are embroidered through the holes and have black beads for "feet" (fig. 1).

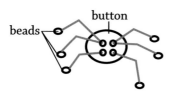

beads   button

Fig. 1

LEAVES POSTCARD

1. Sew the borders onto the background. This give you the opportunity to let some of the fused pieces overlap the borders.

2. Draw a line for the vine on your background fabric with a pencil or chalk marker. Lay three strands of embroidery thread on the drawn line, and sew them with a zigzag stitch.

3. Cut and fuse as many ivy leaves as you like.

PUMPKINS POSTCARD

1. Sew the borders on before applying the shapes. This gives you an opportunity to let shapes overlap the borders.

2. Put as many stars and pumpkins on this postcard as you like. Before fusing the pumpkins, cut away the eyes, nose, and mouth in each one to reveal the dark fabric when the pumpkins are fused to the dark background.

3. Make a spider to hang from the moon in the same way you did for the Ghost postcard.

TRICK-OR-TREAT POSTCARD

1. Cut out all of the letters as indicated in the letter patterns on page 64.

2. Position all of the letters on the background any way you like.

FINISHING TIPS

1. Join the completed postcards according to the SPOOKY NIGHTS! panel assembly diagram.

2. Sew a hanging sleeve to the back of your panel, then date and sign it.

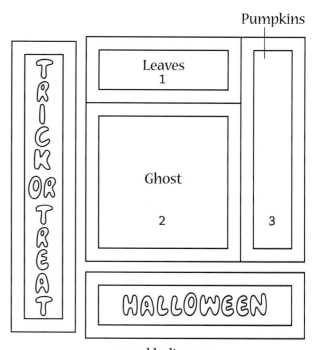

assembly diagram

5 top border

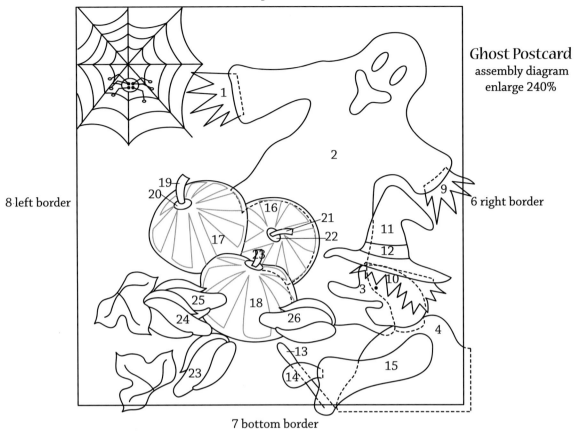

Ghost Postcard
assembly diagram
enlarge 240%

8 left border

6 right border

7 bottom border

Pumpkins

Include the dashed overlap lines
in the individual appliqué pieces.

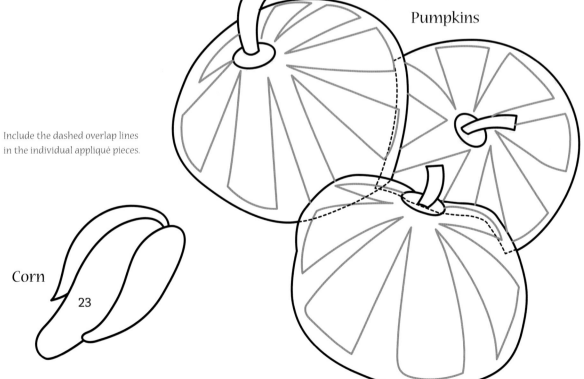

Corn
23

Spider Web

TRICK OR TREAT

3

Trace directly on fusible-web backing.

Include the dashed overlap lines
in the individual appliqué pieces.

Witch

11

12

10

3

4

13

15

14

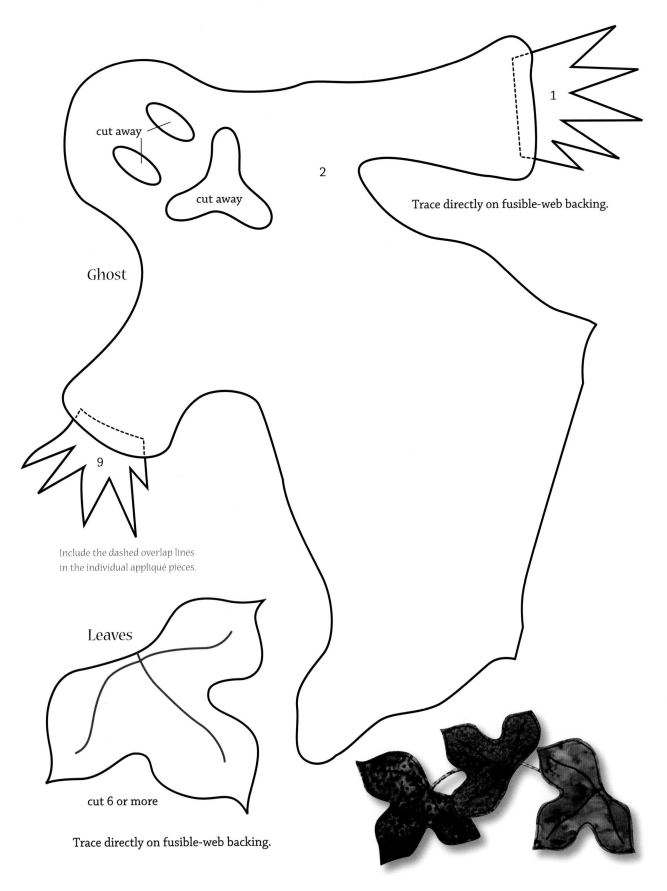

cut away

cut away

1

2

Trace directly on fusible-web backing.

Ghost

9

Include the dashed overlap lines
in the individual appliqué pieces.

Leaves

cut 6 or more

Trace directly on fusible-web backing.

Pumpkins

Cut away mouth and eyes.

HALLOWEEN

cut 1   cut 2   cut 2   cut 2

cut 1   cut 3   cut 1   cut 3

cut 3   cut 1   cut 1   cut 1

full-size letter patterns on pages 77–78

Stars
and
Moon

Trace directly on fusible-web backing.

SEASIDE SPECIAL, 23" x 30". Made by the author.

SEASIDE SPECIAL

panel size: 23" x 30"

REQUIREMENTS

Postcard	Background
Beach Huts	4½" x 15½"
Lighthouse	4½" x 9½"
Cliffs and Sea	4½" x 15½"
Kites	4½" x 9½"
Ice Cream	4½" x 10½"
Fish and Crab	4½" x 10½"
Fishing Boat	Cut 1 rectangle 2½" x 10½" from each of two fabrics. Piece them to make one rectangle 4½" x 10½".
Bucket	4½" x 4½"
Shovel	4½" x 4½"
Sunshine	4½" x 4½"
Windmill	4½" x 4½"

Additional Requirements

Appliqué fabrics. Use sky colors and sea colors for the backgrounds of the landscape and seascape postcards. For the scenes, use a lot of scraps in bright, summery colors. Look at my lobster pots on the Fishing Boat postcard. They were the centers of flowers on an ugly floral fabric

Embellishments. The first thing that catches the quilter's eye is the deck chair pinned on the Beach Huts postcard. I bought this pin many years ago, and it was ideal for this panel. I also used tiny beads for the door handles on this postcard. There are shell-shaped sequins sewn on the Bucket postcard and a small button stitched in the center of the Windmill postcard. On the Fishing Boat postcard, the fishnet is machine stitched with random lines. The seagulls are simple white stitches with a tiny black stitch. Multicolored beads are sewn to one of the ice cream cones, and tiny tied bows are added to the kite strings.

Border strips. Cut borders from 1½" strips.

Top border: Cut background width.

Right-side border: Add 1¼" to background height.

Bottom border: Add 1¼" to background width.

Left-side border: Add 2½" to background height.

Fusible web. Have 1½ yd. on hand.

Batting and Backing. Add 3" to the background measurements for each quilt.

SCRAP BAG OF IDEAS

Here are some other ways to use the SEASIDE SPECIAL postcards as embellishments and banners.
■ The beach huts by themselves are ideal for a wide banner.
■ Sew the ice cream, bucket, and shovel onto a child's sundress or shorts.

CONSTRUCTION TIPS

For general instructions, see Making a Postcard Quilt on pages 6–12.

KITES POSTCARD

1. Trace three copies of the kite template onto a piece of fusible-web backing. Cut the templates, leaving excess allowance around each kite. Fuse one kite template to a solid piece of fabric for kite 1.

2. For kite 2, sew two 2½" x 2½" squares from each of two fabrics. Sew pairs of squares together as shown in figure 1, and align a fusible kite template with the seams, as shown.

3. For kite 3, sew a 1¼" x 3" strip of one fabric to a 2½" strip of another fabric with a ¼" seam allowance. Press the seam allowance open. Position one fusible kite template to the wrong side of your strips, as shown in figure 2. Fuse the template to the fabric and cut out the kite.

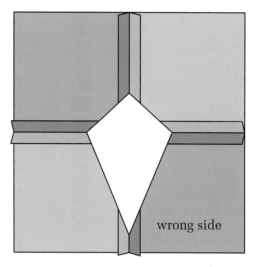

wrong side

Fig. 1

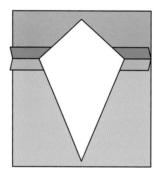

Fig. 2

FISH AND CRAB POSTCARD

1. Cut out as many crabs and fish as you like and place them however you prefer.

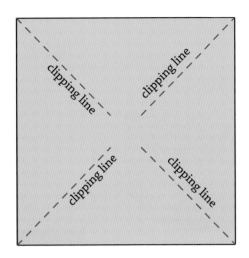

Fig. 3

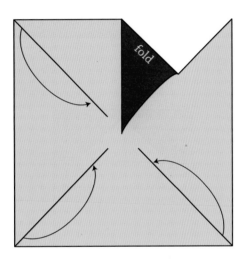

Fig. 4

WINDMILL POSTCARD

1. To make a 3-dimensional windmill, cut one 3½" x 3½" square from each of two brightly colored fabrics, one 3½" x 3½" square of batting, and two 3¼" x 3¼" squares of fusible web.

2. Press a square of fusible web to the wrong side each fabric.

3. Fuse one fabric square to one side of the batting. Then turn the batting over and fuse the second fabric square to the other side of the batting.

4. Trim this sandwich to a 3" x 3" square. Zigzag stitch around the edges of the sandwich, then clip through all three layers as shown by the clipping lines in figure 3.

5. Fold over the corners as shown in figure 4 and tack down the points in the center.

6. Prepare a "blank" postcard by adding the borders, batting, and backing to the Windmill background fabric. Then pin the windmill to the postcard and hand sew tips of windmill to postcard. Tie or sew a button to the center of the windmill.

FINISHING TIPS

1. Join the completed postcards according to the SEASIDE SPECIAL panel assembly diagram on page 69.

2. Sew a hanging sleeve to the back of your panel, then date and sign it.

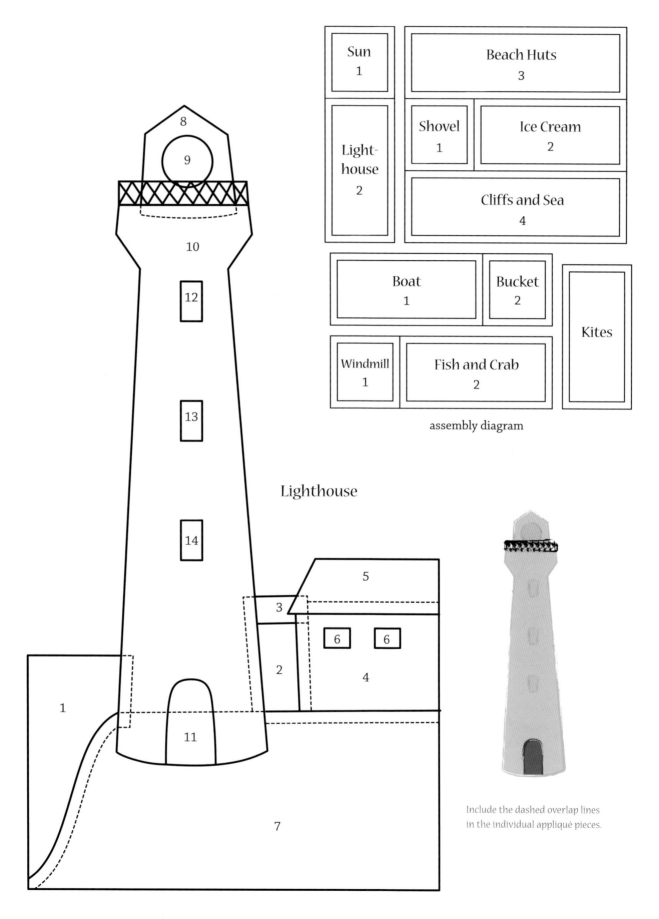

Sun 1	Beach Huts 3
Light-house 2	Shovel 1	Ice Cream 2
	Cliffs and Sea 4

| Boat 1 | Bucket 2 | Kites |
| Windmill 1 | Fish and Crab 2 | |

assembly diagram

Lighthouse

Include the dashed overlap lines
in the individual appliqué pieces.

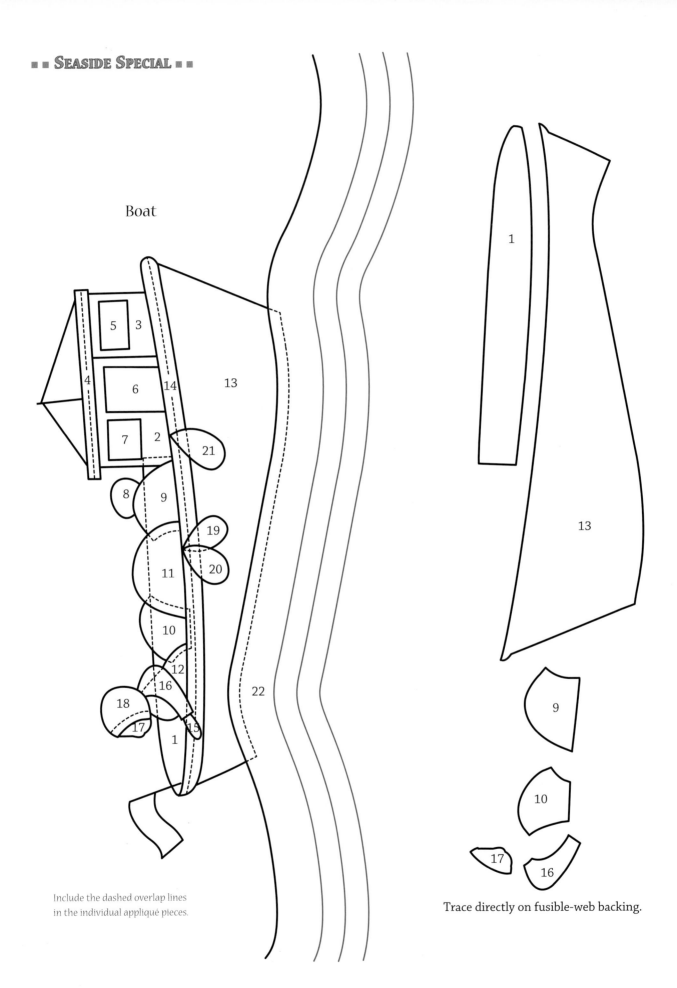

Boat

Include the dashed overlap lines
in the individual appliqué pieces.

Trace directly on fusible-web backing.

Include the dashed overlap lines
in the individual appliqué pieces.

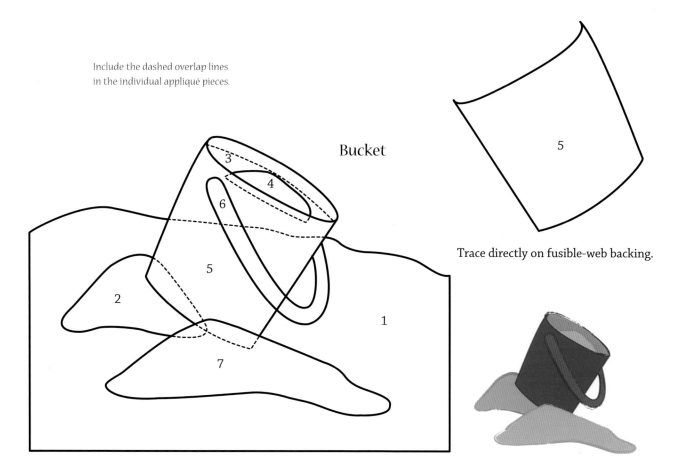

Bucket

5

Trace directly on fusible-web backing.

Shovel

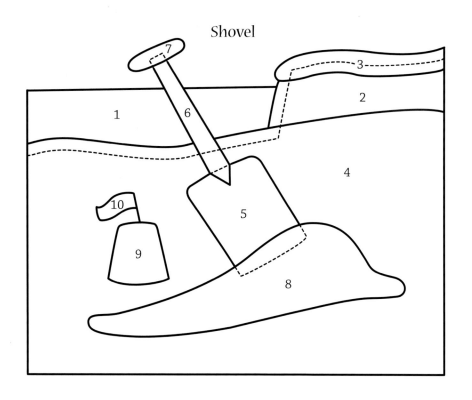

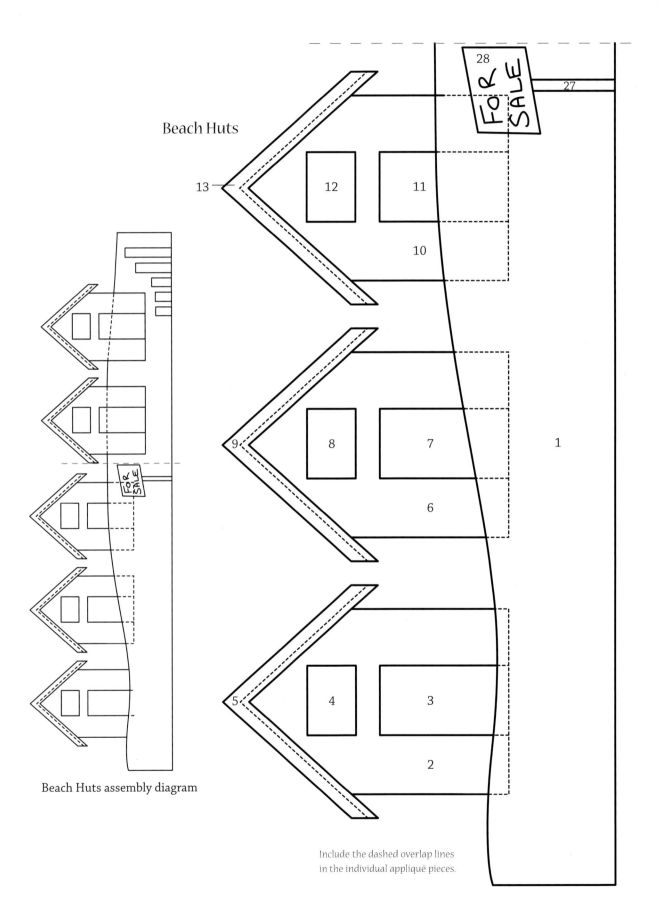

Beach Huts

Beach Huts assembly diagram

Include the dashed overlap lines
in the individual appliqué pieces.

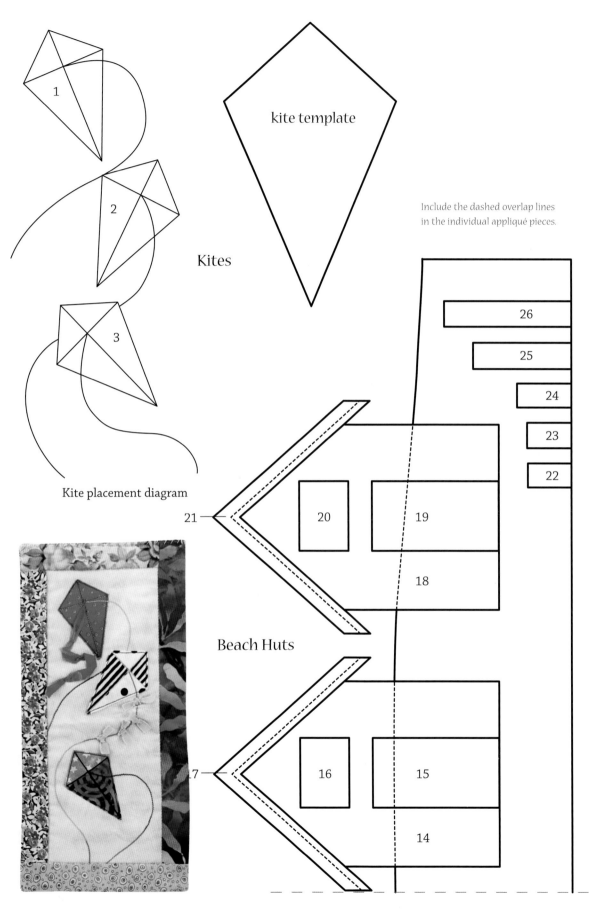

kite template

Kites

Include the dashed overlap lines in the individual appliqué pieces.

Kite placement diagram

Beach Huts

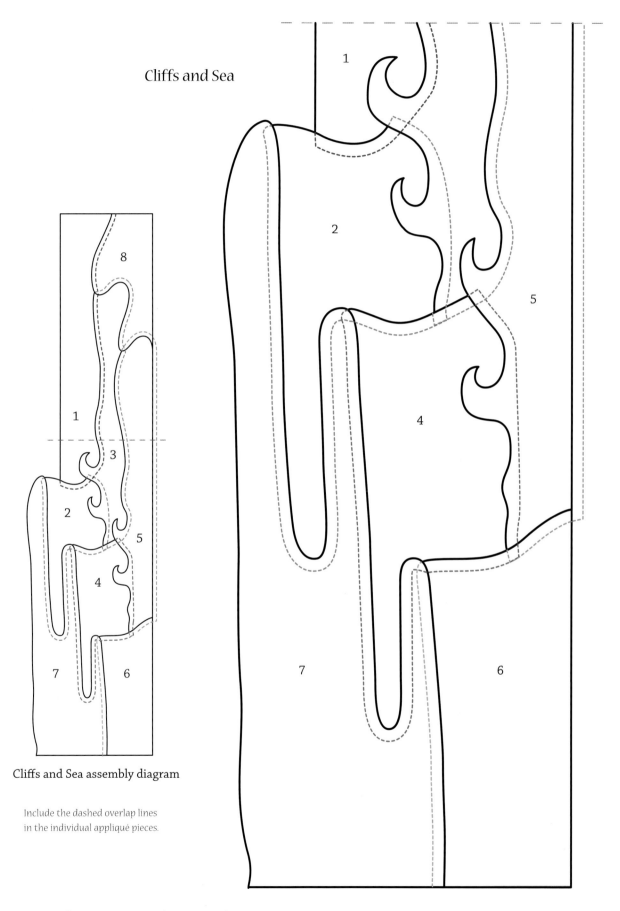

Cliffs and Sea

Cliffs and Sea assembly diagram

Include the dashed overlap lines
in the individual appliqué pieces.

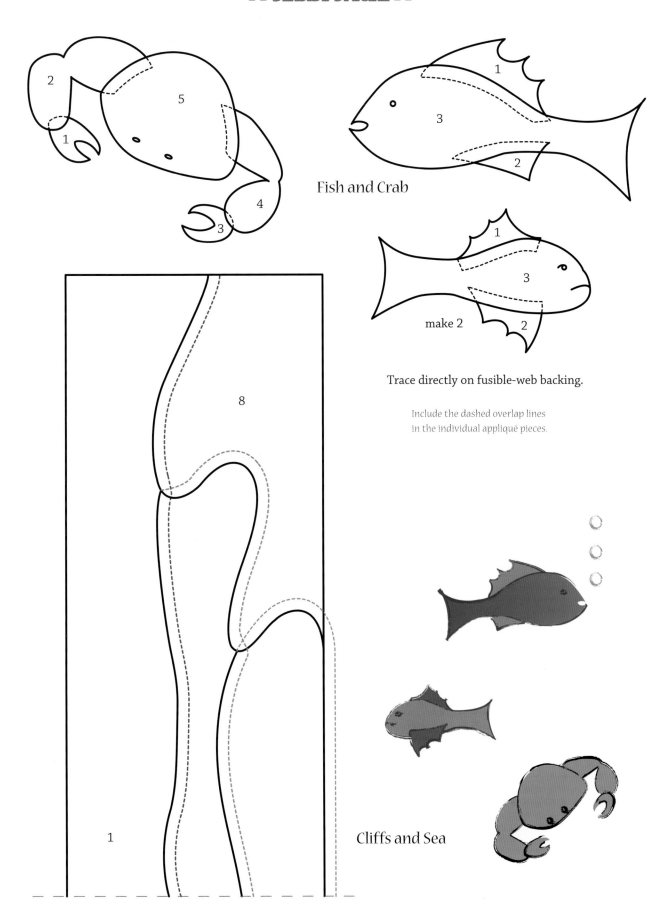

Fish and Crab

make 2

Trace directly on fusible-web backing.

Include the dashed overlap lines
in the individual appliqué pieces.

Cliffs and Sea

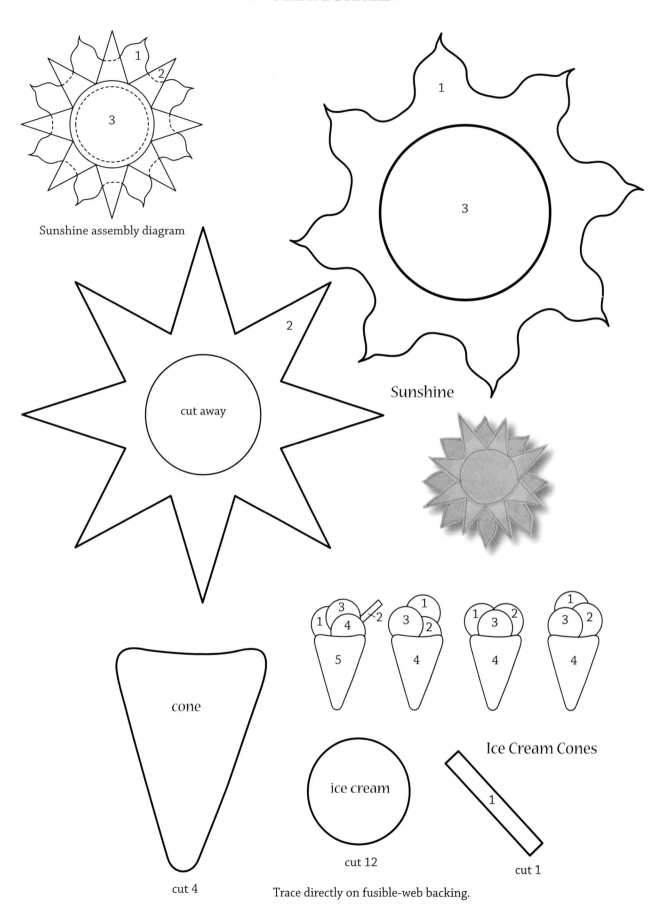

Sunshine assembly diagram

Sunshine

cut away

cone

cut 4

ice cream

cut 12

Ice Cream Cones

cut 1

Trace directly on fusible-web backing.

Meet the Author

Mary started playing with patchwork shapes in the early 1960s, after seeing a friend making a quilt top with hexagons. Having made her own clothes since the age of 14, Mary had accumulated quite a few fabric scraps, along with her old dress patterns. She threw out the dress patterns and started playing with the fabrics. Her first attempt at patchwork was hilarious. She carefully cut out and prepared hundreds of "hexagonal" patches ready to sew together, only to find that they didn't fit as she expected. All of the pieces were, in fact, octagonal! Her next creation was a Log Cabin block, which she describes as "another interesting experiment." This didn't put Mary off, however, and she went on to teach herself the basics. By the early 1980s she was making bed quilts and drawing out her own designs.

Mary has gone on to design and make award-winning quilts and has taught her own designs all over England and Scotland, as well as Canada and the United States. She likes her workshops to be relaxed and enjoyable for her students. Her main aim is to promote quilting and, above all, to show it can be fun. She has worked on many commissioned pieces including two Millennium quilts, and work for Bletchley Park, the code-breaking center during the Second World War. One of Mary's winning quilts is now in The National Postal Museum. Her most recent commission was to make The Quilters' Guild of the British Isles Logo Quilt.

Mary has lived in her home in Eaton Bray, Bedfordshire, England for 46 years with her husband, Peter. He has supported her in every quilting adventure and encouraged her whenever she has had doubts. She has three children, Andrew, Daniel, and Vicky, and two granddaughters, Nell and Grace. Mary's two sisters—one, an identical twin—both take great interest in her career. Mary says that each day is an exciting challenge, some more than others, but she wouldn't change a thing in her life and enjoys every second.

Other AQS Books

This is only a small selection of the books available from the American Quilter's Society. AQS books are known worldwide for timely topics, clear writing, beautiful color photos, and accurate illustrations and patterns. The following books are available from your local bookseller, quilt shop, or public library.

#6904   us$21.95

#7075   us$22.95

#7012   us$19.95

#6903   us$19.95

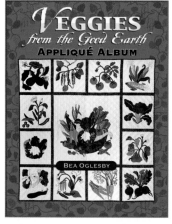

#7017   us$21.95

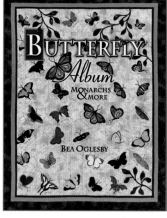

#6674   us$19.95

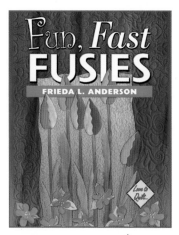

#6801   us$19.95

#6896   us$22.95

#7016   us$22.95

Look for these books nationally.
Call or **Visit** our Web site at

1-800-626-5420
www.AmericanQuilter.com

Mary Mayne

Clever Banners, Panels & Postcards

- **Make whimsical gifts** and decorative banners. Take the postcard craze to new levels with quilts and postcard creations!

- **Fun-filled projects** contain over **60** full-sized appliqué patterns plus a folk art alphabet to personalize your work.

- **Step-by-step guide** for sewing mini-panels into **8** delightful wallhangings— THREE HENS A-LAYING, I ONLY WENT OUT FOR A FAT QUARTER, SEASIDE SPECIAL, and more.

Individually or collectively— these designs are sure to please!

Proudly printed and bound in the **United States of America**

American Quilter's Society

P. O. Box 3290 • Paducah, KY 42002-3290

ISBN 13: 978-1-57432-911-7
ISBN 10: 1-57432-911-1

52195

9 781574 329117

AQS #7010 US$21.95

T2-CYX-911

Navigating *Your* **Future**
Success

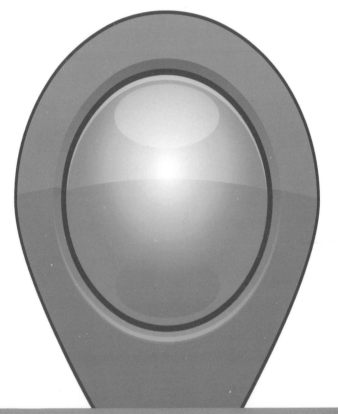

Bruce J. Colbert